WOMEN IN THEIR OWN WORDS

Quotations to Empower and Inspire

Rebecca Foster

summersdale

WOMEN IN THEIR OWN WORDS

Summersdale Publishers Ltd
46 West Street
Chichester
West Sussex
PO19 1RP
UK

www.summersdale.com

Printed and bound in the Czech Republic

ISBN: 978-1-84953-854-1

Substantial discounts on bulk quantities of Summersdale books are available to corporations, professional associations and other organisations. For details contact Nicky Douglas by telephone: +44 (0) 1243 756902, fax: +44 (0) 1243 786300 or email: nicky@summersdale.com.

Introduction

Words have the power to change our lives. This book brings together the thoughts of great writers, political pioneers, enchanting actors, historical wits, successful entrepreneurs, modern pop stars, passionate feminists and champions of human dignity – all of them female, and all of them with unique insights to share. No matter when or where they originated, these are words to empower us right now, and to inspire us wherever we go.

THERE ARE TWO WAYS OF SPREADING LIGHT:
TO BE THE CANDLE OR THE MIRROR
THAT REFLECTS IT.

EDITH WHARTON

No one can make
you feel inferior without
your consent.

ELEANOR ROOSEVELT

I don't want
other people
to decide who
I am. I want to
decide that
for myself.

EMMA WATSON

One child, one teacher, one pen and one book can change the world.

MALALA YOUSAFZAI

GENTLE LADIES, YOU WILL REMEMBER
TILL OLD AGE WHAT WE DID TOGETHER
IN OUR BRILLIANT YOUTH!

SAPPHO

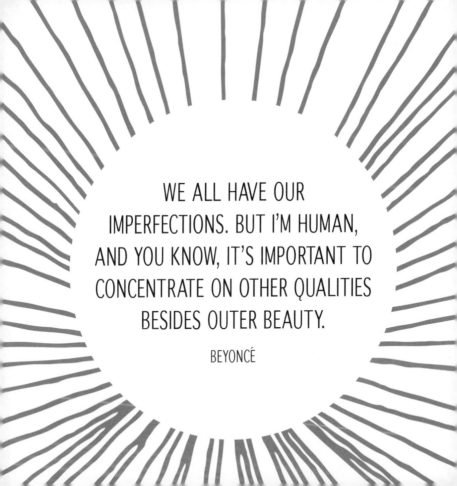

WE ALL HAVE OUR
IMPERFECTIONS. BUT I'M HUMAN,
AND YOU KNOW, IT'S IMPORTANT TO
CONCENTRATE ON OTHER QUALITIES
BESIDES OUTER BEAUTY.

BEYONCÉ

USE EACH INTERACTION

TO BE THE BEST,
MOST POWERFUL
VERSION OF YOURSELF.

MARIANNE WILLIAMSON

TRY TO BE A RAINBOW
IN SOMEONE'S CLOUD.

MAYA ANGELOU

YOU HAVE TO BELIEVE IN YOURSELF
WHEN NO ONE ELSE DOES – THAT MAKES
YOU A WINNER RIGHT THERE.

VENUS WILLIAMS

The **control** and understanding of our personal **fears** is one of the most important **undertakings** of our lives.

HELEN MIRREN

Women are
the largest
untapped reservoir
of talent
in the world.

HILLARY CLINTON

If I **waited** for **perfection**... I would **never** write a word.

MARGARET ATWOOD

LIFE APPEARS TO ME TOO SHORT
TO BE SPENT IN NURSING ANIMOSITY,
OR REGISTERING WRONGS.

CHARLOTTE BRONTË

NEVER REGRET. IF IT'S GOOD,
IT'S WONDERFUL. IF IT'S BAD,
IT'S EXPERIENCE.

ELEANOR HIBBERT

THINK YOU SHOULD TAKE YOUR JOB SERIOUSLY, BUT NO
URSELF - THAT IS THE BEST COMBINATION. I THINK YO
OULD TAKE YOUR JOB SERIOUSLY, BUT NOT YOURSELF
AT IS THE BEST COMBINATION. I THINK YOU SHOULD TAK
UR JOB SERIOUSLY, BUT NOT YOURSELF - THAT IS TH
ST COMBINATION. I THINK YOU SHOULD TAKE YOUR JO
RIOUSLY, TAKE YOUR JOB SERIOUSLY, BUT NOT YOURSELF
AT IS THE BEST COMBINATION. BUT NOT YOURSELF - I THIN
U SHOULD TAKE THAT IS THE BEST COMBINATION. YOUR JO
RIOUSLY, BUT NOT YOURSELF - THAT IS THE BEST COMBINATIO
HINK YOU SHOULD JUDI DENCH TAKE YOUR JOB SERIOUSL
T NOT YOURSELF - THAT IS THE BEST COMBINATION. I THIN
U SHOULD TAKE YOUR JOB SERIOUSLY, BUT NOT YOURSEL
THAT IS THE BEST COMBINATION. I THINK YOU SHOULD TAK
UR JOB SERIOUSLY, BUT NOT YOURSELF - THAT IS THE BES
MBINATION. I THINK YOU SHOULD TAKE YOUR JOB SERIOUSL

...E IMPORTANT THING IS NOT WHAT THEY THINK OF ME, E
WHAT I THINK OF THEM. THE IMPORTANT THING IS NOT WH
THEY THINK OF ME, BUT WHAT I THINK OF THEM. THE IMPORTA
THING IS NOT WHAT THEY THINK OF ME, BUT WHAT I THINK
THEM. THE IMPORTANT THING IS NOT WHAT THEY THINK OF
BUT WHAT I THINK IS NOT WHAT OF THEM. THE IMPORTA
THING IS NOT WHAT THEY THINK OF ME, BUT WHAT I THINK
THEM. THE IMPORTANT BUT WHAT I THINK OF THEM. TH
S NOT WHAT THEY THINK OF ME, BUT WHAT I THINK OF TH
HE IMPORTANT QUEEN VICTORIA NOT WHAT THEY THINK
ME, BUT WHAT I THINK OF THEM. THE IMPORTANT THING IS N
WHAT THEY THINK OF ME, BUT WHAT I THINK OF THEM. T
IMPORTANT THING IS NOT WHAT THEY THINK OF ME, BUT WHA
THINK OF THEM. THE IMPORTANT THING IS NOT WHAT THEY TH
OF ME, BUT WHAT I THINK OF THEM. THE IMPORTANT THING
OT WHAT THEY THINK OF ME, BUT WHAT I THINK OF TH

I WANT TO TELL ANY YOUNG GIRL OUT THERE
WHO'S A GEEK, I WAS A REALLY SERIOUS GEEK
IN HIGH SCHOOL. IT WORKS OUT.

SHERYL SANDBERG

Everyone's dream can come true if you just stick to it and work hard.

SERENA WILLIAMS

Life is a succession
of lessons
which must
be lived
to be understood.

HELEN KELLER

I don't **care** what
is **written** about me
so long as it isn't **true**.

DOROTHY PARKER

I DWELL IN POSSIBILITY.

EMILY DICKINSON

BEAUTY IS PERFECT IN ITS IMPERFECTIONS, SO YOU JUST HAVE TO GO WITH THE IMPERFECTIONS.

DIANE VON FÜRSTENBERG

MY FEARS CAME TRUE:
PEOPLE CALLED ME FAT
AND HIDEOUS, AND I LIVED.
AND NOW I KEEP LIVING.

LENA DUNHAM

I KNOW I HAVE
THE BODY BUT
OF A WEAK AND
FEEBLE WOMAN;
BUT I HAVE THE
HEART AND
STOMACH OF
A KING, AND
OF A KING OF
ENGLAND TOO.

QUEEN ELIZABETH I

IF YOU DON'T LIKE SOMETHING, CHANGE IT.
IF YOU CAN'T CHANGE IT, CHANGE YOUR
ATTITUDE. DON'T COMPLAIN.

MAYA ANGELOU

I would venture to guess that Anon, who wrote so many poems without signing them, was often a woman.

VIRGINIA WOOLF

You're only

young once,

but you can

be immature

forever.

GERMAINE GREER

The most common
way people give up their
power is by thinking they
don't have any.

ALICE WALKER

ABOVE ALL, BE THE HEROINE
OF YOUR LIFE, NOT THE VICTIM.

NORA EPHRON

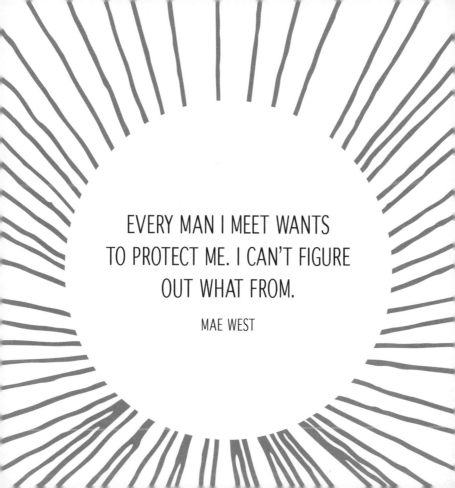

EVERY MAN I MEET WANTS
TO PROTECT ME. I CAN'T FIGURE
OUT WHAT FROM.

MAE WEST

A GIRL
SHOULD BE
TWO THINGS:
WHO AND
WHAT SHE WANTS.

COCO CHANEL

SOMEBODY'S NEGATIVITY DUMPED ON YOU
IS A BIGGER COMMENTARY ON HOW THEY
FEEL ABOUT THEMSELVES THAN YOU.

KELLY RIPA

Take **advantage** of every opportunity that comes your way, with **grace** and humility. Be a sponge – and **absorb** and learn.

CHITA RIVERA

Don't play a
supporting
role in your
own life.

ROBIN ROBERTS

Speak! It's a revolution for women to have **voices.**

JILL SOLOWAY

THE TROUBLE WITH SOME WOMEN IS
THEY GET ALL EXCITED ABOUT NOTHING –
AND THEN THEY MARRY HIM.

CHER

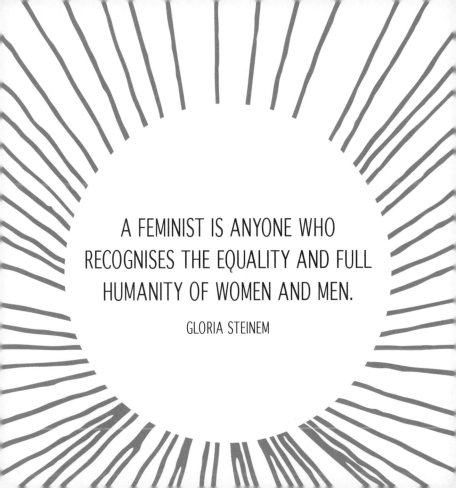

A FEMINIST IS ANYONE WHO
RECOGNISES THE EQUALITY AND FULL
HUMANITY OF WOMEN AND MEN.

GLORIA STEINEM

EN A WOMAN BECOMES HER OWN BEST FRIEND LIFE I.
SIER. WHEN A WOMAN BECOMES HER OWN BEST FRIEND LIF
EASIER. WHEN A WOMAN BECOMES HER OWN BEST FRIEN
E IS EASIER. WHEN A WOMAN BECOMES HER OWN BEST FRIEN
E IS EASIER. WHEN A WOMAN WHEN A WOMAN BECOMES HE
N BEST BECOMES HER OWN BEST FRIEND LIFE IS EASIER. WH
N BEST FRIEND LIFE IS EASIER. WHEN A WOMAN BECOME
END LIFE IS EASIER. WHEN A WOMAN BECOMES HER OW
ST FRIEND LIFE IS EASIER. DIANE VON FÜRSTENBERG WHEN
MAN BECOMES HER OWN BEST FRIEND LIFE IS EASIER. WHE
WOMAN BECOMES HER OWN BEST FRIEND LIFE IS EASIER
EN A WOMAN BECOMES HER OWN BEST FRIEND LIFE I
SIER. WHEN A WOMAN BECOMES HER OWN BEST FRIEND LIF
EASIER. WHEN A WOMAN BECOMES HER OWN BEST FRIEN
E IS EASIER. WHEN A WOMAN BECOMES HER OWN BEST
END LIFE IS EASIER. WHEN A WOMAN BECOMES HER OWN BEST

DO NOT WISH [WOMEN] TO HAVE POWER OVER MEN, BUT OV
HEMSELVES. I DO NOT WISH [WOMEN] TO HAVE POWER OV
IEN; BUT OVER THEMSELVES. I DO NOT WISH [WOMEN] TO HA
OWER OVER MEN; BUT OVER THEMSELVES. I DO NOT W
WOMEN] TO HAVE POWER OVER MEN; BUT OVER THEMSELVE
O NOT WISH [WOMEN] TO HAVE POWER OVER MEN; BUT OV
HEMSELVES. I DO NOT WISH [WOMEN] TO HAVE POWER OV
IEN; BUT OVER TO HAVE POWER OVER MEN; THEMSELVES. I
OT WISH [WOMEN] TO BUT OVER THEMSELVES. HAVE POV
VER MEN; BUT OVER THEMSELVES. I DO NOT WISH [WOM
O HAVE POWER OVER MEN; MARY WOLLSTONECRAFT BUT OV
HEMSELVES. I DO NOT WISH [WOMEN] TO HAVE POWER OV
IEN; BUT OVER THEMSELVES. I DO NOT WISH [WOMEN] TO HA
OWER OVER MEN; BUT OVER THEMSELVES. I DO NOT W
WOMEN] TO HAVE POWER OVER MEN; BUT OVER THEMSELVE
O NOT WISH [WOMEN] TO HAVE POWER OVER MEN; BUT OV

FITTING IN IS BORING.
BUT IT TAKES YOU NEARLY YOUR
WHOLE LIFE TO WORK THAT OUT.

CLARE BALDING

Nothing in life is to be feared, it is only to be understood. Now is the time to understand more, so that we may fear less.

MARIE CURIE

It's better to
look ahead
and prepare than
to look back
and regret.

JACKIE JOYNER-KERSEE

Treating women with respect should not be contingent on whether or not it 'gets you somewhere'.

LINDY WEST

THE MOST VALUABLE COMMODITY IN
BUSINESS TODAY, IF PEOPLE WOULD ONLY
RECOGNISE IT, IS ENTHUSIASM.

RONA JAFFE

I NEVER LOSE SIGHT OF THE
FACT THAT JUST BEING IS FUN.

KATHARINE HEPBURN

YOU DON'T KNOW

A WOMAN UNTIL
YOU HAVE HAD
A LETTER FROM HER.

ADA LEVERSON

IN A TIME OF DESTRUCTION,
CREATE SOMETHING.

MAXINE HONG KINGSTON

LOVE AND KINDNESS
GO HAND IN HAND.

MARIAN KEYES

Women, like men, should try to do the **impossible.** And when they fail, their **failure** should be a challenge to others.

AMELIA EARHART

The more you practise,
the better.
But in any case,
practise more
than you play.

BABE DIDRIKSON ZAHARIAS

One hour of right-down
love is worth an age
of dully living on.

APHRA BEHN

WE ARE NOT INTERESTED
IN THE POSSIBILITIES OF DEFEAT;
THEY DO NOT EXIST.

QUEEN VICTORIA

YOUR VICTORY IS RIGHT
AROUND THE CORNER.
NEVER GIVE UP.

NICKI MINAJ

DARE TO BE AS PHYSICALLY ROBUST AND VARIED AS YOU ALWAYS WERE.

SUSIE ORBACH

BE BRUTALLY FRANK WITH
YOURSELF. IT'S SAFER.

NELLIE BLY

PERSONAL SIZE AND MENTAL SORROW HAVE
CERTAINLY NO NECESSARY PROPORTIONS.
A LARGE BULKY FIGURE HAS AS GOOD A RIGHT
TO BE IN DEEP AFFLICTION, AS THE MOST
GRACEFUL SET OF LIMBS IN THE WORLD.

JANE AUSTEN

I don't focus on what I'm up against. I focus on my goals and I try to ignore the rest.

VENUS WILLIAMS

We ask ourselves,
'Who am I to be
brilliant, gorgeous, talented,
fabulous?'
Actually, who are you
not to be?

MARIANNE WILLIAMSON

We are the hero
of our own story.

MARY McCARTHY

MANY RECEIVE ADVICE,
ONLY THE WISE PROFIT FROM IT.

HARPER LEE

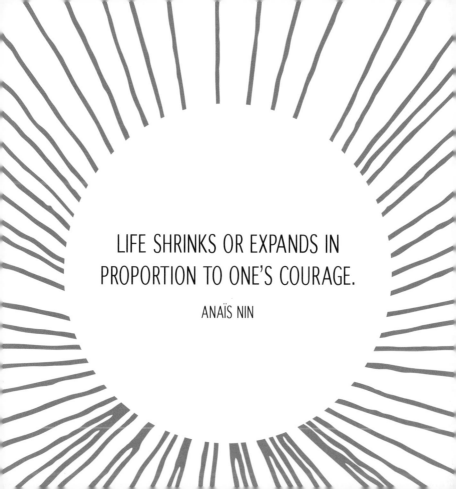

LIFE SHRINKS OR EXPANDS IN
PROPORTION TO ONE'S COURAGE.

ANAÏS NIN

IT'S ABOUT
FOCUSING
ON THE
FIGHT AND
NOT THE
FRIGHT.

ROBIN ROBERTS

LOCK UP YOUR LIBRARIES IF YOU LIKE; BUT THERE IS NO GATE, NO LOCK, NO BOLT THAT YOU CAN SET UPON THE FREEDOM OF MY MIND.

VIRGINIA WOOLF

IT IS NOT GOOD TO
CROSS THE BRIDGE BEFORE
YOU GET TO IT.

JUDI DENCH

Memories of our lives, of our works and our deeds will continue in others.

ROSA PARKS

Love largely and
hate nothing.
Hold no aim that
does not chord
with universal good.

ELLA WHEELER WILCOX

Obtain power, then, by all means; power is the law of man; make it yours.

MARIA EDGEWORTH

I THINK ONE'S FEELINGS WASTE THEMSELVES IN WORDS; THEY OUGHT ALL TO BE DISTILLED INTO ACTIONS, AND INTO ACTIONS WHICH BRING RESULTS.

FLORENCE NIGHTINGALE

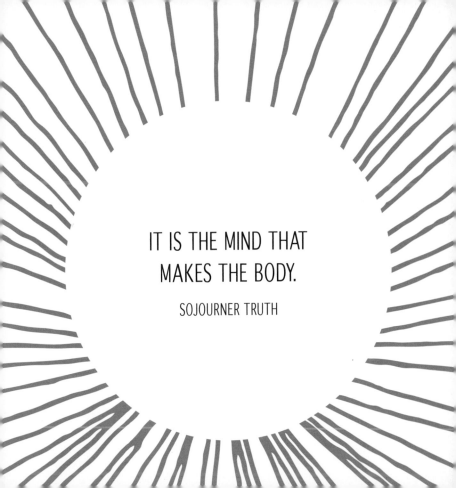

IT IS THE MIND THAT
MAKES THE BODY.

SOJOURNER TRUTH

...E EDUCATION SHOULD EDUCATE US OUT OF SELF INT

METHING FAR FINER; INTO A SELFLESSNESS WHICH LINKS U

TH ALL HUMANITY. REAL EDUCATION SHOULD EDUCATE U

T OF SELF INTO SOMETHING FAR FINER; INTO A SELFLESSNES

ICH LINKS US WITH ALL HUMANITY. REAL EDUCATION SHOUL

JCATE US REAL EDUCATION SHOULD EDUCATE OUT OF SEL

O SOMETHING US OUT OF SELF INTO SOMETHING FAR FINEF

O A SELFLESSNESS FAR FINER; INTO A SELFLESSNESS WHIC

KS US WHICH LINKS US WITH ALL HUMANITY. WITH AL

MANITY. REAL EDUCATION SHOULD EDUCATE US OUT OF SEL

O SOMETHING FAR FINER; NANCY ASTOR INTO A SELFLESSNES

ICH LINKS US WITH ALL HUMANITY. REAL EDUCATION SHOUL

JCATE US OUT OF SELF INTO SOMETHING FAR FINER; INT

ELFLESSNESS WHICH LINKS US WITH ALL HUMANITY. REA

JCATION SHOULD EDUCATE US OUT OF SELF INTO SOMETHIN

FINER; INTO A SELFLESSNESS WHICH LINKS US WITH AL

THOUGH HE HAD EDEN TO LIVE IN, MAN CANNOT BE HAPPY ALONE. THOUGH HE HAD EDEN TO LIVE IN, MAN CANNOT BE HAPPY ALONE. THOUGH HE HAD EDEN TO LIVE IN, MAN CANNOT BE HAPPY ALONE. THOUGH HE HAD EDEN TO LIVE IN, MAN CANNOT BE HAPPY ALONE. THOUGH HE HAD EDEN TO LIVE IN, MAN CANNOT BE HAPPY ALONE. THOUGH HE HAD EDEN TO LIVE IN, **THOUGH HE HAD** MAN CANNOT BE HAPPY ALONE. THOUGH HE HAD EDEN TO LIVE IN, MAN CANNOT BE HAPPY ALONE. THOUGH **MAN CANNOT BE HAPPY ALONE.** HE HAD EDEN TO LIVE IN, MAN CANNOT BE HAPPY ALONE. THOUGH HE HAD EDEN TO LIVE IN, MAN **JOSEPHINE POLLARD** CANNOT BE HAPPY ALONE. THOUGH HE HAD EDEN TO LIVE IN, MAN CANNOT BE HAPPY ALONE. THOUGH HE HAD EDEN TO LIVE IN, MAN CANNOT BE HAPPY ALONE. THOUGH HE HAD EDEN TO LIVE IN, MAN CANNOT BE HAPPY ALONE. THOUGH HE HAD EDEN TO LIVE IN, MAN CANNOT BE HAPPY ALONE. THOUGH HE HAD ED

YOU MAY NOT CONTROL ALL THE EVENTS
THAT HAPPEN TO YOU, BUT YOU CAN DECIDE
NOT TO BE REDUCED BY THEM.

MAYA ANGELOU

Don't spend **time** beating on a **wall,** hoping to transform it into a **door.**

COCO CHANEL

Not many men have both
good fortune
and good sense.

MARILYN FRENCH

Don't be like **anyone** else. **Find** your voice, your script, your **rhythms.**

JILL SOLOWAY

LOVE IS AN INDESCRIBABLE
SENSATION – PERHAPS A CONVICTION,
A SENSE OF CERTITUDE.

JOYCE CAROL OATES

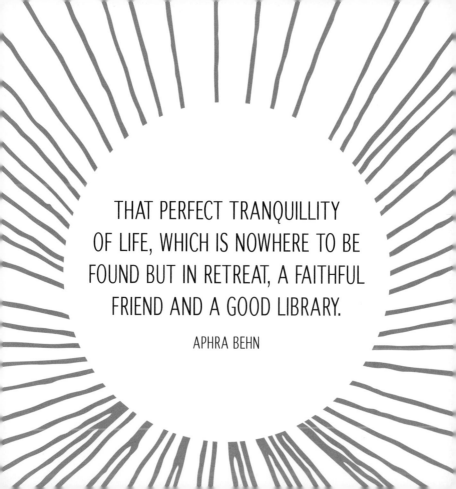

THAT PERFECT TRANQUILLITY
OF LIFE, WHICH IS NOWHERE TO BE
FOUND BUT IN RETREAT, A FAITHFUL
FRIEND AND A GOOD LIBRARY.

APHRA BEHN

VIRTUE CAN ONLY FLOURISH
AMONGST EQUALS.

MARY WOLLSTONECRAFT

A WORD
AFTER A
WORD AFTER
A WORD IS
POWER.

MARGARET ATWOOD

ENERGY RIGHTLY APPLIED
AND DIRECTED WILL
ACCOMPLISH ANYTHING.

NELLIE BLY

Not knowing **when** the dawn will come, I **open** every door.

EMILY DICKINSON

Feminism is
the ability
to choose what you
want to do.

NANCY REAGAN

I am not afraid;
I was born to do this.

JOAN OF ARC

THE FIRST PROBLEM FOR ALL
OF US, MEN AND WOMEN, IS NOT
TO LEARN, BUT TO UNLEARN.

GLORIA STEINEM

YOU DON'T GET SOMETHING FOR
NOTHING AND YOU HAVE TO WORK
HARD FOR WHAT YOU WANT IN LIFE.

SARAH STOREY

NOBILITY,

WITHOUT VIRTUE,
IS A FINE SETTING
WITHOUT A GEM.

JANE PORTER

THERE CAN BE NO HAPPINESS
IF THE THINGS WE BELIEVE
IN ARE DIFFERENT FROM THE
THINGS WE DO.

FREYA STARK

THERE IS NO COSMETIC
FOR BEAUTY LIKE HAPPINESS.

MARGUERITE GARDINER

In science, all facts, no matter how trivial or banal, enjoy democratic equality.

MARY McCARTHY

All adventures,
especially
into new territory,
are scary.

SALLY RIDE

You can't **win** them all —
but you can **try**.

BABE DIDRIKSON ZAHARIAS

SUDDENLY WHEN ONE HAS ALMOST
MADE UP ONE'S MIND TO A CERTAIN
ACTION IT CASUALLY THROWS AN
OPPORTUNITY INTO ONE'S PATH.

ELEANOR HIBBERT

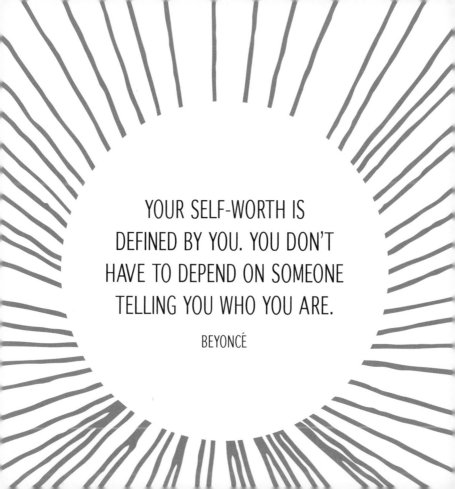

YOUR SELF-WORTH IS
DEFINED BY YOU. YOU DON'T
HAVE TO DEPEND ON SOMEONE
TELLING YOU WHO YOU ARE.

BEYONCÉ

DO YOUR THING

AND DON'T CARE
IF THEY LIKE IT.

TINA FEY

THE TRICK IN LIFE IS
LEARNING HOW TO
DEAL WITH IT.

HELEN MIRREN

THERE IS NO CHARM EQUAL
TO TENDERNESS OF HEART.

JANE AUSTEN

All I can do is **follow** my instincts, because I'll never **please** everyone.

EMMA WATSON

Give back in
some way.
Always be
thoughtful
of others.

JACKIE JOYNER-KERSEE

It is **justice,** not charity, that is wanting in the **world.**

MARY WOLLSTONECRAFT

THERE MUST BE A BATTLE, A BRAVE
BOISTEROUS BATTLE, WITH PENNANTS
WAVING AND CANNON ROARING, BEFORE
THERE CAN BE PEACEFUL TREATIES AND
ENTHUSIASTIC SHAKING OF HANDS.

MARY ELIZABETH BRADDON

BE LESS CURIOUS ABOUT PEOPLE
AND MORE CURIOUS ABOUT IDEAS.

MARIE CURIE

IMISM CAN BE RELEARNT. OPTIMISM CAN BE RELEA
TIMISM CAN BE RELEARNT. OPTIMISM CAN BE RELEARN
PTIMISM CAN BE RELEARNT. OPTIMISM CAN BE RELEAR
E RELEARNT. OPTIMISM CAN BE RELEARNT. OPTIMISM
N BE RELEARNT. OPTIMISM CAN BE RELEARNT. OPTIMISM CA
RELEARNT. OPTIMISM OPTIMISM CAN BE RELEARNT. OPTIMI
TIMISM CAN BE CAN BE RELEARNT. OPTIMISM CAN B
EARNT. OPTIMISM RELEARNT. CAN BE RELEARNT. OPTIMIS
RELEARNT. OPTIMISM CAN BE RELEARNT. OPTIMISM CA
RELEARNT. OPTIMISM MARIAN KEYES CAN BE RELEARN
TIMISM CAN BE RELEARNT. OPTIMISM CAN BE RELEARN
EARNT. OPTIMISM CAN BE RELEARNT. OPTIMISM CA
RELEARNT. OPTIMISM CAN BE RELEARNT. OPTIMISM CAN B
EARNT. OPTIMISM CAN BE RELEARNT. OPTIMISM CA
E RELEARNT. OPTIMISM CAN BE RELEARNT. OPTIMISM CA
AN BE RELEARNT. OPTIMISM CAN BE RELEARNT. OPTIMI

UDE IS EVERYTHING. ATTITUDE IS EVERYTHING. ATTITUDE
DE IS EVERYTHING. ATTITUDE IS EVERYTHING. ATTITUDE
TTITUDE IS EVERYTHING. ATTITUDE IS EVERYTHING. ATTITU
EVERYTHING. ATTITUDE IS EVERYTHING. ATTITUDE IS EV
EVERYTHING. ATTITUDE IS EVERYTHING. ATTITUDE IS EVE
DE IS EVERYTHING. ATTITUDE IS EVERYTHING. ATTITUDE
TTITUDE IS EVERYTHING. ATTITUDE IS EVERYTHING. ATTITU
DE IS EVERYTHING. ATTITUDE IS EVERYTHING. ATTITUDE IS
EVERYTHING. ATTITUDE IS EVERYTHING. ATTITUDE IS EV
TTITUDE IS EVERYTHING. DIANE VON FÜRSTENBERG ATTITUDE
TTITUDE IS EVERYTHING. ATTITUDE IS EVERYTHING. ATTITU
VERYTHING. ATTITUDE IS EVERYTHING. ATTITUDE IS EVE
TTITUDE IS EVERYTHING. ATTITUDE IS EVERYTHING. ATTI
TTITUDE IS EVERYTHING. ATTITUDE IS EVERYTHING. ATTITU
EVERYTHING. ATTITUDE IS EVERYTHING. ATTITUDE IS EVE
TTITUDE IS EVERYTHING. ATTITUDE IS EVERYTHING. ATTITU

CEASE TELLING OTHER HUMAN BEINGS
WHAT THEY 'SHOULD' AND 'SHOULDN'T'
DO WITH THEIR BODIES.

LINDY WEST

I never hanker after the past — I prefer to devote myself to new tasks.

STEFFI GRAF

If you obey all
the rules,
you miss all
the fun.

KATHARINE HEPBURN

I declare to you that woman must not depend upon the protection of man, but must be taught to protect herself, and there I take my stand.

SUSAN B. ANTHONY

IN ORDER TO BE IRREPLACEABLE ONE
MUST ALWAYS BE DIFFERENT.

COCO CHANEL

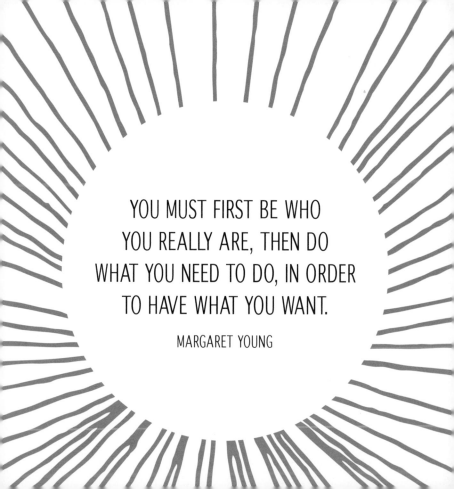

YOU MUST FIRST BE WHO
YOU REALLY ARE, THEN DO
WHAT YOU NEED TO DO, IN ORDER
TO HAVE WHAT YOU WANT.

MARGARET YOUNG

I THINK IF YOU FEEL LIKE
YOU WERE BORN TO WRITE,
THEN YOU PROBABLY WERE.

LENA DUNHAM

NOTHING IS
IMPOSSIBLE,
THE WORD
ITSELF
SAYS 'I'M
POSSIBLE'!

AUDREY HEPBURN

FORGIVENESS IS A
VIRTUE OF THE BRAVE.

INDIRA GANDHI

You can be **strong** and
true to yourself without
being rude or **loud.**

PAULA RADCLIFFE

We must believe that
we are gifted
for something, and
that this thing,
at whatever cost, must
be attained.

MARIE CURIE

We should all **start** to live before we get too old. Fear is **stupid.** So are regrets.

MARILYN MONROE

I HAVE LEARNED OVER THE YEARS
THAT WHEN ONE'S MIND IS MADE UP,
THIS DIMINISHES FEAR.

ROSA PARKS

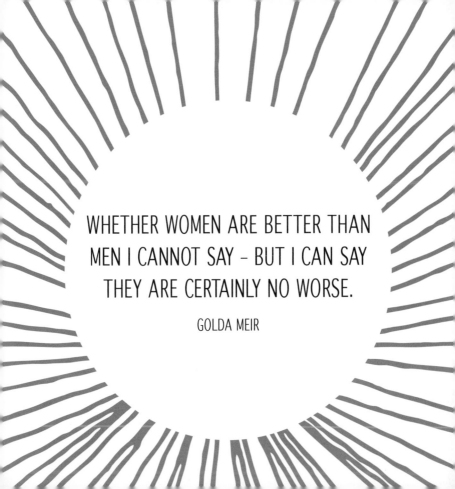

WHETHER WOMEN ARE BETTER THAN MEN I CANNOT SAY – BUT I CAN SAY THEY ARE CERTAINLY NO WORSE.

GOLDA MEIR

I AM NOT BOUND TO
GIVE REASONS FOR WHAT
I DO TO ANYBODY.

LADY HESTER STANHOPE

LIFE-FULFILLING

WORK IS NEVER ABOUT
THE MONEY – WHEN YOU
FEEL TRUE PASSION FOR
SOMETHING, YOU INSTINCTIVELY
FIND WAYS TO NURTURE IT.

EILEEN FISHER

YOU CAN STAND TALL WITHOUT
STANDING ON SOMEONE. YOU CAN BE
A VICTOR WITHOUT HAVING VICTIMS.

HARRIET WOODS

The most **effective** way
to **do it** is to do it.

AMELIA EARHART

Think like a queen. A queen
is not afraid
to fail. Failure is another
stepping stone
to greatness.

OPRAH WINFREY

Women need **real** moments of solitude and **self-reflection** to balance out how much of ourselves we **give** away.

BARBARA DE ANGELIS

THE CONNECTIONS BETWEEN AND AMONG
WOMEN ARE THE MOST FEARED, THE MOST
PROBLEMATIC, AND THE MOST POTENTIALLY
TRANSFORMING FORCE ON THE PLANET.

ADRIENNE RICH

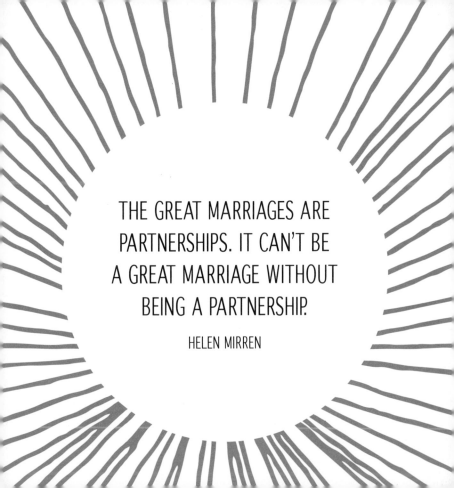

THE GREAT MARRIAGES ARE
PARTNERSHIPS. IT CAN'T BE
A GREAT MARRIAGE WITHOUT
BEING A PARTNERSHIP.

HELEN MIRREN

E OF US ARE BECOMING THE MEN WE WANTED
RRY. SOME OF US ARE BECOMING THE MEN WE WANTE
MARRY.SOME OF US ARE BECOMING THE MEN WE WAN
NTED TO MARRY. SOME OF US ARE BECOMING THE MEN W
NTED TO MARRY. SOME OF US ARE BECOMING THE ME
E WANTED TO MARRY. SOME OF US ARE BECOMING TH
N WE WANTED TO ARE BECOMING THE MEN MARRY. SOME
ARE BECOMING THE MEN WE WANTED TO MARRY. SOME
COMING THE MEN WE WANTED TO MARRY. SOME OF U
US ARE BECOMING THE MEN GLORIA STEINEM WE WANTED
ME OF US ARE BECOMING THE MEN WE WANTED TO MARR
ECOMING THE MEN WE WANTED TO MARRY. SOME OF U
E BECOMING THE MEN WE WANTED TO MARRY. SOME
ARE BECOMING THE MEN WE WANTED TO MARRY. SON
E MEN WE WANTED TO MARRY. SOME OF US ARE BECOMIN
COMING THE MEN WE WANTED TO MARRY. SOME OF

HEY SAY THAT WOMEN TALK TOO MUCH. IF YOU HAVE WORK
N CONGRESS YOU KNOW THAT THE FILIBUSTER WAS INVENT
Y MEN. THEY SAY THAT WOMEN TALK TOO MUCH. IF Y
ORKED IN CONGRESS YOU KNOW THAT THE FILIBUSTER W
NVENTED THEY SAY THAT WOMEN TALK TOO MUCH. BY M
HEY SAY THAT IF YOU HAVE WORKED IN CONGRESS WOM
ALK TOO MUCH. YOU KNOW THAT THE FILIBUSTER IF YOU HA
ORKED IN CONGRESS WAS INVENTED BY MEN. YOU KN
HE FILIBUSTER WAS INVENTED BY MEN. THEY SAY THAT WOM
ALK TOO MUCH. IF YOU CLARE BOOTHE LUCE HAVE WORK
ONGRESS YOU KNOW THAT THE FILIBUSTER WAS INVENT
EN. THEY SAY THAT WOMEN TALK TOO MUCH. IF YOU HA
ORKED IN CONGRESS YOU KNOW THAT THE FILIBUSTER W
NVENTED BY MEN. THEY SAY THAT WOMEN TALK TOO MU
YOU HAVE WORKED IN CONGRESS YOU KNOW THAT T
LIBUSTER WAS INVENTED BY MEN. THEY SAY THAT WOMEN TA

IT IS THE ULTIMATE LUXURY TO
COMBINE PASSION AND CONTRIBUTION.
IT'S ALSO A VERY CLEAR PATH TO HAPPINESS.

SHERYL SANDBERG

My choice, my responsibility. Win or lose, only I hold the key to my destiny.

ELAINE MAXWELL

Yet if a woman never lets herself go, how will she ever know how far she might have got?

GERMAINE GREER

When the **whole** world is silent, even one voice becomes **powerful.**

MALALA YOUSAFZAI

THE BEST AND MOST BEAUTIFUL THINGS IN THE
WORLD CANNOT BE SEEN OR EVEN TOUCHED –
THEY MUST BE FELT WITH THE HEART.

HELEN KELLER

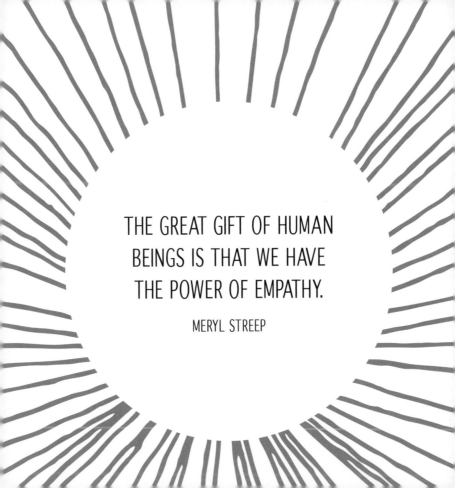

THE GREAT GIFT OF HUMAN
BEINGS IS THAT WE HAVE
THE POWER OF EMPATHY.

MERYL STREEP

ART

IS AN EXPRESSION
OF WHO WE ARE,
WHAT WE BELIEVE, AND
WHAT WE DREAM ABOUT.

JULIANNE MOORE

THERE IS NO DEFINITION OF
BEAUTY, BUT WHEN YOU CAN SEE
SOMEONE'S SPIRIT COMING THROUGH,
SOMETHING UNEXPLAINABLE, THAT'S
BEAUTIFUL TO ME.

LIV TYLER

THE MOST IMPORTANT THING IS
TO ENJOY YOUR LIFE - TO BE HAPPY -
IT'S ALL THAT MATTERS.

AUDREY HEPBURN

I've always **loved** the idea of not being what people **expect** me to be.

DITA VON TEESE

You must find a

new way

to think before you

can master

a new way to be.

MARIANNE WILLIAMSON

I am no bird; and no net
ensnares me; I am a free
human being with an
independent will.

CHARLOTTE BRONTË

TAKING JOY IN LIFE IS A
WOMAN'S BEST COSMETIC.

ROSALIND RUSSELL

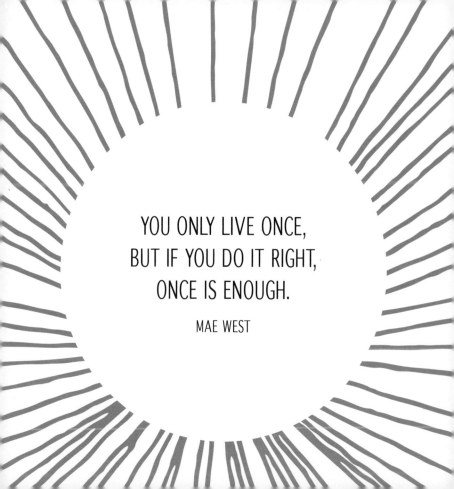

YOU ONLY LIVE ONCE,
BUT IF YOU DO IT RIGHT,
ONCE IS ENOUGH.

MAE WEST

THERE'S POWER IN LOOKING SILLY AND NOT CARING THAT YOU DO.

AMY POEHLER

TO SUCCEED YOU HAVE TO
BELIEVE IN SOMETHING WITH
SUCH A PASSION THAT IT
BECOMES A REALITY.

ANITA RODDICK

A WOMAN WITH A VOICE IS BY
DEFINITION A **STRONG WOMAN. BUT
THE SEARCH TO FIND THAT VOICE CAN
BE REMARKABLY DIFFICULT.**

MELINDA GATES

Far away there in the sunshine are my highest aspirations. I may not reach them, but I can look up and see their beauty, believe in them, and try to follow where they lead.

LOUISA MAY ALCOTT

How wonderful it is that
nobody need
wait a single moment
before starting
to improve the world.

ANNE FRANK

The giving of **love** is an
education in itself.

ELEANOR ROOSEVELT

EACH PERSON MUST LIVE THEIR LIFE
AS A MODEL FOR OTHERS.

ROSA PARKS

IF EVERYTHING WAS PERFECT,
YOU WOULD NEVER LEARN AND
YOU WOULD NEVER GROW.

BEYONCÉ

ATTEMPT THE
IMPOSSIBLE
IN ORDER TO
IMPROVE
YOUR WORK.

BETTE DAVIS

YOU CAN BREAK THAT
BIG PLAN INTO SMALL
STEPS AND TAKE THE
FIRST STEP RIGHT AWAY.

INDIRA GANDHI

NEVER GIVE UP, FOR THAT IS
JUST THE PLACE AND TIME THAT
THE TIDE WILL TURN.

HARRIET BEECHER STOWE

Choose people who lift you up.

MICHELLE OBAMA

Every **great dream** begins
with a dreamer.
Always remember,
you have within you
the **strength**,
the patience, and the
passion to reach
for the **stars**
to change the world.

HARRIET TUBMAN

Forever is composed of nows.

EMILY DICKINSON

If you're interested in finding out more about our books, find us on Facebook at **Summersdale Publishers** and follow us on Twitter at **@Summersdale**.

www.summersdale.com